Contents

RICS guidance notes

RICS guidance notes provide assistance to RICS members on aspects of professional practice. Where procedures are recommended for specific professional tasks within this guidance note, these are intended to reflect good practice for these tasks.

This guidance note aims to set out the recommended content for a residential building survey. Additional services can always be offered. The content suggested is that which is considered suitable to provide a comprehensive assessment of a residential property. The scope of the building survey service may vary from case to case but will be determined by the specific Terms and Conditions of Engagement as agreed between the surveyor and the client.

The guidance note is prepared bearing in mind it could be read by students or inexperienced surveyors as well as the more experienced. It is not meant to be prescriptive but the surveyor should appreciate the benefit of following a methodical approach.

Surveyors are not required to follow the advice and recommendations contained in this guidance note. They should, however, note the following points:

- When an allegation of professional negligence is made against a surveyor, the court is likely to take account of the contents of any relevant guidance notes published by RICS in deciding whether or not the surveyor has acted with reasonable competence.

- In the opinion of RICS, a member conforming to the practices recommended in this guidance note ought to have at least a partial defence to an allegation of negligence by virtue of having followed these practices. However, members have the responsibility of deciding when it is appropriate to follow the guidance. If it is followed in an inappropriate case, the member will not be exonerated merely because the recommendations were found in an RICS guidance note.

- On the other hand, it does not follow that a member will be adjudged negligent if he or she has not followed the practices recommended in this guidance note. It is for each individual surveyor to decide on the appropriate procedure to follow in any professional task. However, where members depart from the practice recommended in this guidance note, they should do so only for good reason. In the event of litigation, the court may require them to explain why they decided not to adopt the recommendations contained within this guidance note. A failure to comply with this guidance note does not necessarily of itself constitute negligence.

- In addition, guidance notes are relevant to professional competence in that each surveyor should be up-to-date and should have become familiar with their scope and application within a reasonable time after their publication.

1   Introduction

This guidance note has been prepared for the purpose of providing chartered surveyors with a source of information and guidance in respect of residential building surveys.

This guidance note is written to apply to England and Wales, although much of its content is equally applicable elsewhere. It is operative from March 2004, from which date the RICS publication *Building Surveys of Residential Property – A Guidance Note for Surveyors*, published in 1996, ceases to be RICS guidance.

General guidance of this nature cannot cover all circumstances and each property should be assessed on an individual basis having regard to the specific needs of the client. The guidance offered is considered adaptable for all types of residential property. It is accepted that surveyors may well have good reasons for not following all the aspects of this guidance note. It is for the surveyor to decide upon such issues depending on the individual circumstances, e.g. nature of construction or site conditions.

RICS is concerned to ensure that members should only hold themselves out to be competent in fields for which their training and background experience are appropriate and relevant. It is important that the surveyor undertaking residential building surveys has relevant experience in this field, has appropriate knowledge of building construction, and is sufficiently skilled to inspect and report on the particular property involved.

Surveyors providing residential building surveys and associated services are advised to:

- assess the needs of the client;

- consider the extent of any investigations to be made, advise on the limitations of the agreed inspection and obtain instructions from the client for any additional services required;

- undertake an impartial and professional assessment of the property and its condition, and report to the client in the detail and style necessary to provide a balanced professional opinion to the extent required by the agreed instructions; and

- comply with the agreed instructions, which should have been confirmed in writing and which are the basis of the contract between the client and the surveyor.

2 Pre-inspection procedures

It is important to ensure that there is a good level of communication with the client from the outset. The surveyor is advised to make every endeavour to speak to the client prior to the inspection in order to clarify precise requirements and to avoid possible misunderstandings. It is worth remembering that clients' expectations of surveys may be unrealistically high and that clients may not be familiar with the range of survey options that the surveyor will be able to offer. For this reason, clients will generally require advice on the type and extent of the survey and report needed and when required this advice should be given freely, without charge. The surveyor is advised to provide a comparison between the various levels of service that could be offered, in order that the distinctions may be clearly understood by the client. Surveyors are recommended to ensure that they have a good working knowledge of the building survey service in order to explain the key features and benefits.

2.1 Enquiry

When receiving an enquiry, it is recommended that all reasonable steps are taken to assess the needs of the prospective client so that the surveyor provides the most appropriate service. The surveyor is advised to ask sufficient questions so that an informed offer to carry out the building survey can be made. Questions should seek to establish, where appropriate:

- name, address and contact arrangements of prospective client;
- name and telephone number of agents (if any) for access;
- price being paid for the property;
- involvement of lender;
- age, type and construction of building (if known);
- general particulars of the property;
- tenure (if known);
- extent of inspection required of main building;
- extent of inspection required of outbuildings, facilities and grounds;
- whether the property is vacant or occupied;
- extent and nature of any specialist tests;
- any restrictions to access;
- purpose for which survey is required;
- proposed use;
- nature of any special instructions or requirements;
- nature of any works proposed;
- nature of any specific client concerns;
- number of visits client has made to property;
- number of copies of report required;

- timing and method of delivery of report;

- availability of client for decisions during survey; and

- other local considerations.

At this stage surveyors are recommended to ensure they are fully acquainted with the client's requirements and have the necessary skills and resources to complete the survey task.

2.2 Offer and acceptance of instructions

In law, a contract is created by an offer and acceptance between parties who want to enter into a legally binding relationship. Valuable consideration also needs to pass between the parties to bring the contract into effect.

Contract made

The surveyor is likely to have been telephoned by a potential client in the first instance, and in such cases it is open to the surveyor to set out the basis of any contract before the end of this conversation. The surveyor is advised to make it clear that the contract itself will be on the terms of a letter or form that will be sent to the client.

Once the scope of the surveyor's work is contractually established it may not be changed without the client's agreement. If terms are not properly agreed and recorded before any work is carried out disputes are much more likely.

The surveyor should promptly confirm in writing the client's instructions, including the terms and conditions under which the service is to be provided. This is best executed by a Letter of Confirmation or Order Form which should include a statement to be signed by the client confirming that he or she has received, read and understood the Terms and Conditions of Engagement. The surveyor's confirmation should also refer to the scope and standard of the work to be done, repeating particulars about the property, where relevant, on which the fee is based and should include the following additional information:

- the Terms and Conditions of Engagement;

- clarification of any limitations and restrictions;

- extent of any agreed additional services;

- extent of any agreed specialist testing;

- fee agreed or quoted showing VAT where appropriate;

- terms of payment;

- likely inspection date and report delivery date;

- Letter of Confirmation/Order Form for signature and return by client;

- arrangements in respect of handling complaints.

2.3 Desk study

The surveyor is advised to carry out a desk study which, ideally, should be carried out before the site visit. This is to ensure that the surveyor has all the necessary background information to enable professional assessments to be made on site. In certain instances it may not be possible to obtain some information until after the inspection.

The surveyor may consider the following information, if available:

- estate agents' particulars;

- relevant site information, e.g. the nature of subsoils;

- particular exposure to wind driven rain, or frost attack;

- details of previous works and permissions;

- guarantees, warranties and any supporting reports, specifications and quotations;

- conservation area status;

- listed building status;

- lease details (see Appendix A: Leasehold residential property); and

- any other technical reports relating to the property (for background information only, not for reliance) unless otherwise agreed.

The above list of information is not intended as a full list of all the information that may be required and it is for the surveyor to consider local conditions and obtain any information relevant to the particular circumstances of the case.

Even where the surveyor has built up a good working knowledge of the type of property concerned and its locality, a structured approach to the desk study is recommended. Sources of material may include the internet as well as more traditional means. It is recommended that the sources of all information provided are stated, where appropriate, in the report.

3 Terms and Conditions of Engagement

3.1 The Terms and Conditions of Engagement should attempt to address relevant aspects in respect of the service to be provided. The following matters should be included within the **particulars**:

- the client's name and address,
- the surveyor's name and business address,
- the property address,
- the purpose of the report,
- details of any special instructions,
- the likely inspection date,
- the likely report delivery date,
- the number of copy reports to be provided,
- the agreed fee,
- any additional fees,
- the payment date,
- the signature(s) of the client(s) to confirm acceptance of the Terms and Conditions of Engagement.

3.2 The **specific terms** should include:

- a description of the property to be inspected;
- additional services (if applicable), e.g. testing of services, additional investigation, arboricultural report, costed estimates for repairs, market valuation, insurance rebuilding cost assessment;
- special terms agreed (if applicable).

3.3 The **general terms** of engagement should:

- introduce the purpose of the service;
- indicate the content of the report;
- indicate the method for delivery of the report;
- set out the payment terms;
- clarify the standard assumptions that will be made;
- set out the scope of the inspection, and the extent to which elements and services will be inspected;
- clarify the visual nature of the inspection, and accessibility constraints;
- clarify how areas that could not be inspected will be dealt with;
- indicate the extent of inspection in relation to flats or maisonettes;
- clarify how environmental and other related issues will be dealt with;

- set out the assumptions made in relation to hazardous materials and ground conditions;

- set out the assumptions made in relation to legal searches and local authority approvals;

- indicate how miscellaneous matters will be dealt with;

- set out the arrangements for the handling of complaints;

- clarify the confidentiality of the report and the extent to which the client or the client's professional advisors may rely upon it.

3.4 Appendix B to this guidance note provides example Terms and Conditions of Engagement which are capable of use with or without amendment, as may be agreed between the parties to suit the circumstances of the particular case.

Copies of the example Terms and Conditions of Engagement contained in Appendix B may be purchased in quantity from RICS Books.

4   Inspection

4.1   General principles

It is advisable that surveyors carrying out building surveys identify, where possible, the construction and materials which have been used in the property under inspection. Unless a surveyor has been able to identify the particular construction and materials used in the property, he or she may not be able to report upon the likely consequences of any failures found.

4.2   Health and safety aspects

It is recommended that the surveyor be sufficiently fit to be able to undertake the task, particularly in relation to gaining access to voids that may be present within the property, and that he or she considers health and safety aspects, e.g. the need to:

- make a record of the appointment either at the office or at home and let someone know the expected return time;

- carry a personal alarm;

- carry a mobile phone or pager;

- use ladders and other equipment safely;

- refer to *Surveying Safely* on the RICS website (http://www.rics.org/resources/surveying_safely/index.html).

4.3   Equipment

It is recommended that the surveyor should have available the following equipment:

- equipment for recording findings, e.g. paper, pens or pencils;

- small tape measure or measuring rod;

- binoculars or telescope;

- compass;

- 3 metre ladder;

- hard hat;

- spirit level;

- plumb bob;

- mask, particularly for loft spaces and inspection chambers where there is a greater likelihood of contaminants;

- crack gauge, or ruler;

- electronic moisture meter;

- torches;

- camera, with flash;

- claw hammer and bolster;

- lifting equipment for standard inspection chamber covers;

- screwdriver, bradawl or hand-held probe;

- mirror;

- meter cupboard key;

- means of determining inclination of roof pitch;

- first-aid kit;

- means of personal identification.

A variety of optional equipment should also be considered (e.g. where additional services are being offered):

- moisture meter accessories such as a surface temperature probe, a humidity sensor, an air temperature sensor;

- deep insulated probes;

- a long tape measure;

- additional screwdrivers;

- a hand-held metal detector;

- a marble;

- an adjustable set square;

- a boroscope;

- a magnifying glass;

- spare batteries and bulbs;

- protective overalls and gloves.

The surveyor should ensure that he or she has all the equipment reasonably necessary to carry out the survey required.

Care should be taken to ensure that moisture meters are maintained in a good working condition and that calibration checks are made in accordance with manufacturers' requirements.

4.4 Oral enquiries of the owner or occupier

Information may be available from the property owner, occupier or, where the property is vacant, the owner's agent about matters affecting the property. It is advised that this is used as a guide. However, it is worth remembering that information supplied may not be entirely accurate, but the primary purpose of this procedure is to assist the surveyor in establishing matters of relevance and to follow a trail of prudent enquiry. For example, the available information from the owner or occupier may include or relate to:

- previous structural repairs (e.g. underpinning or strengthening), past/current insurance claims;

- structural alterations or additions;

- redecoration or renewal of finishes;

- local authority or statutory approvals;

- the age of the property;

- how long the owner has occupied the property;

- whether the property is listed or located in a conservation area;

- guarantees or warranties (e.g. in respect of timber or damp treatment, cavity wall tie replacement, etc.);

- neighbour or other disputes affecting the property;

- availability of mains services – details of maintenance/service records, especially for gas and electrical installations;

- private services;

- status of roadways (adopted or private);

- known rights of way or other rights that may exist over the property or benefit the property;

- tenure;

- confirmation of selling price (where separate valuation advice is being given);

- the location of any concealed traps and hatches that may provide access to parts of the structure;

- specific questions that may arise as a result of the surveyor needing to follow a reasonable trail of enquiry;

- if leasehold – lease term (original and unexpired), ground rent, service charge, insurance arrangements, responsibility for repairs and maintenance, and the identity of the freeholders or superior landlord and the management company;

- ownership of boundaries;

- *Party Wall* Act issues;

- if private drainage – type thereof and locations of holding tanks, plant and equipment, when/how serviced, capacity of holding tanks, and frequency of emptying in relation to the number of persons in household;

- whether the property or immediate locality has been affected by flooding.

4.5 Inspection, note taking and reflective thought

Within the scope of the Terms and Conditions of Engagement the surveyor is responsible for carefully and thoroughly inspecting the property and recording the construction and defects that are evident. The surveyor is therefore recommended to accept that it is his or her responsibility, within the limits of the agreed instructions, to see as much of the property as is physically accessible. For most properties, however, a full inspection is prevented by physical conditions. If so, it is recommended that an explanation is provided. In such cases the surveyor might need to make a professional assessment based upon what can be inspected and advise upon the likelihood or otherwise of a defect or defects being present. In some situations this may lead to the surveyor recommending the need for further opening-up or investigation works.

Surveyors are advised to develop a logical sequence of inspection and it is essential that all relevant parts of the property are inspected as closely as possible and their inter-relationship considered. For example, the structural frame also includes the interdependence of roof framing, walls and intermediate floors. It is recommended that the surveyor assesses the overall performance of the structural elements so that they are not taken in isolation.

It is essential for the surveyor to take and keep a permanent record of the site notes made at the time of inspection. In addition to written notes the surveyor may include sketch plans, diagrams and photographs. The notes should record the construction, condition and circumstances of inspection and should indicate the checks made to the fabric and structure and what was found.

The surveyor is advised not to limit the time for inspection but should take the time required for the property in question.

Before the report is written, it is essential that the surveyor allows sufficient time for reflective thought. The surveyor is reminded not to attempt to write the report during the inspection but to prepare it from notes after appropriate consideration.

5 The report

5.1 The report should:

- be clearly presented, in a logical order, and written in plain language in such a way that it may be easily understood by the client. It is recommended that technical expressions be kept to a minimum and, where necessary, explained in lay terms;

- be factual wherever possible and unambiguous;

- be seen to differentiate between fact and the surveyor's opinion;

- provide a balanced view of the property and describe individual elements in sufficient detail to identify their construction, condition and location.

It is recommended that each element of the property be separately addressed and described, the sequence depending upon the logical format adopted.

5.2 In respect of each section of the construction and services, it is advised that, where relevant, the report narrative:

- describes the form of construction and materials used for each element;

- outlines the performance characteristics of the material or construction;

- describes obvious defects;

- describes the identifiable risk of potential or hidden defects;

- outlines remedial options;

- if considered to be significant, explains the likely consequences of non-repair;

- makes general recommendations in respect of the likely timescale for necessary work;

- includes, where appropriate, recommendation for further investigation prior to commitment to purchase;

- cross-refers to the surveyor's overall assessment where necessary;

- identifies the nature of risks in areas which have not been inspected.

5.3 Because the building survey report is intended to reflect the considered professional opinion of the surveyor, the edges between inspection, diagnosis and reporting often overlap, and so for the purpose of practical guidance these related elements have not been treated entirely separately. The following section, *Suggested report contents*, sets out the issues that surveyors are advised to consider and take into account when reporting to the client in the context of a building survey. Each of the elements shown below are explained in greater detail, together with a suggested approach for surveyors, under the following headings:

- Introduction

- Description of the property

- Location

- Surveyor's overall assessment

- Construction and condition – structural frame, exterior and interior

- Services

- Environmental and other issues

- Outbuildings, grounds and boundaries

- Matters for legal advisor's attention

- Additional services

It is important to emphasise, however, that because buildings are sufficiently different, it is for the surveyor to decide upon the appropriateness of report headings, or the sequence in which they are followed, to suit the individual property.

6 Suggested report contents

6.1 Introduction

6.1.1 *Scope of instructions*

It is advised that the scope of the instructions are stated, to clarify, for example, whether the report is intended to cover the whole property, or is limited to a single issue or to a group of issues. Reference may need to be made to the Terms and Conditions of Engagement within which the inspection and report are to be undertaken, and a copy of these can be provided as an appendix to the report. It is recommended that any variations found necessary on inspection are stated. In order to minimise exposure to third party claims, it is common to include the following clause:

> 'This report is for the private and confidential use of [add name of the client] for whom the report is undertaken and should not be reproduced in whole or part or relied upon by third parties with the exception of […] for any use without the express written authority of the surveyor(s).'

6.1.2 *Property address*

Include the full correct postal address together with the postcode.

6.1.3 *Client's name and address*

The name and address of the client, and any other information supplied (such as fax or email address), may be given. Where instructions are received through a legal adviser or other third party, this should be stated, and the report should be sent addressed to the client care of that third party.

6.1.4 *Date of survey*

It is advised that the date or dates of the actual inspection are stated, not the date of typing or word processing the report.

6.1.5 *Weather*

Reference may need to be made to the weather at the time of inspection and to the characteristics of the preceding period.

6.1.6 *Limitations of inspection*

Surveyors are advised to provide a clear statement of the limitations posed by the building or its occupation. These limitations are additional to any imposed in the conditions of engagement and are a consequence of both the building and the circumstances of the inspection. These are therefore additional items that are drawn to the attention of the client and may include, for example:

- extent of fitted floor coverings;
- extent to which the property was furnished;
- areas where the amount of stored goods is heavy;

- areas to which access was not granted;

- exceptional limitations (e.g. due to snow, parked vehicles, building work, dogs, babies).

6.1.7 *Information relied upon in this report*

As part of the referencing, the surveyor is recommended to undertake a desk study (see 2.3 Desk study) and make appropriate enquiries, either verbal or written, of the owner (see 4.4 Oral enquiries of the owner or occupier). The outcome of these enquiries together with the source of information are reported in this section.

6.2 Description of the property

6.2.1 *Type and age*

A thumbnail description of the property is recommended, including its:

- ✓ type,

- general design,

- principal elements of construction,

- ✓ approximate age,

- apparent age of any extensions, substantial modifications or conversion works,

- listed status, and

- current use.

The estimates of age should be as accurate as possible and sources of information should be stated.

6.2.2 *Accommodation*

It is advised that the accommodation is listed in brief, showing the current use of main rooms and circulation areas broken down by floor levels. The surveyor is advised to review the accommodation and its layout; assess modernisations and alterations and review the building in respect of general habitability. If the property is a flat or maisonette, the storey upon which it is situated and the number of storeys in the block should be reported. Detailed measurements are not usually reported but the surveyor is recommended to note and, as appropriate, report any design features or dimensions that are important to the use and enjoyment of the property.

6.2.3 *Tenure and occupation*

It is recommended that the nature of the interest and the source of information are stated, e.g. 'I understand from the seller/selling agent that the property is offered for sale on a freehold basis with vacant possession'. For leasehold or other tenure the surveyor is advised to state the unexpired term of years, amount of rent (ground, chief, fixed, variable, etc.), and the approximate maintenance or service charge. The report may need to mention that the lease may impose repairing obligations on the lessee (see Appendix A: Leasehold residential property). It should be noted whether or not the lease has been inspected.

6.2.4 *Further comments*

Further issues not covered elsewhere in this section can be included here.

6.3 **Location**

6.3.1 *Location*

Here the surveyor is advised to provide a brief opinion of the main features affecting the use and enjoyment of the property which are either evident from the inspection or known to the surveyor. The position of the property within the road and the general character of the immediate neighbourhood should be described. If it is known that the property is situated within (or adjacent to) a conservation area, this may need to be stated.

6.3.2 *Orientation*

It may be helpful to state the approximate compass direction the front of the property faces, e.g. south, or south-east. (The front of the property would typically be the elevation containing the principal entrance door.)

6.3.3 *The site and surrounding areas*

A general description of the main physical features of the site should be provided to include its general topography and layout. It is recommended that advice is given where the site is sloping or, for example, located adjacent to or within an area having an obvious risk of flooding or erosion. The likely nature of the ground conditions (e.g. subsoils, the presence of springs or culverts, or mining activity) may need to be described where these could have an effect upon the condition of the property, its outbuildings or services.

6.3.4 *Local factors*

The surveyor is advised to consider the general condition, construction, design and perceived use of adjoining properties, in order to identify and report any special factors (e.g. significant nuisances), which may have an adverse effect upon the subject property.

6.3.5 *Trees and hedges*

A general description should be given of any trees or hedges that could have an effect upon the condition of the property, its outbuildings or services. Any significant risk of structural damage from tree roots should be identified.

6.4 **Surveyor's overall assessment**

6.4.1 *Surveyor's overall opinion*

It is recommended that the surveyor aims to provide the client with a clear summary of the property and its main positive and negative features. This comprises an overview of the key issues which may include:

- the nature of the property, its construction and its design;

- the adequacy of the structural framework and fabric;

- adequacy of services;

- a comparison of the condition of the subject property with others of similar age and style;

- conformity with modern requirements;

- the likely scale of maintenance required; and

- special client requirements.

6.4.2 *Areas of concern*

Any main areas of concern other than in respect of condition, whether related to site location, design, structural framework, fabric or services, nature of construction, or planning should be recorded, noting any defect that could be the subject of a claim under a buildings insurance policy.

6.4.3 *Summary of repairs*

The surveyor is advised to list, or provide in the form of an appendix, a summary of the main repair items and to cross-reference these to the main body of the report.

6.4.4 *Cost guidelines*

(For use only where the service as agreed with the client includes cost guidelines.)

It is undoubtedly of value to a client to receive an estimate of the cost of recommended remedial works but if this is given the surveyor is advised to state, at some length, the reservations and limitations of such advice. It is recommended that the client is informed, for example, of the need to obtain formal quotations prior to a legal commitment to purchase the property.

In such cases, the surveyor is recommended to provide an overall budget cost guide for main defects, including where appropriate separate figures for exceptional items of repair and allowing for VAT and for costs of professional or local authority fees as relevant.

6.4.5 *Further investigations*

In the event that the surveyor considers it necessary for areas of the property to be opened up to establish its true condition, it is recommended that this is stated clearly in the report. Recommendations for specialist tests, for example, in respect of service installations, should only be made where the surveyor is uncertain as to the true condition. The need for such tests to be undertaken before legal commitment to purchase should be stated within the report.

6.5 **Construction and condition – structural frame, exterior and interior**

6.5.1 *Constructional principles*

The surveyor is recommended, where relevant, to:

- assess and describe how the building performs structurally, for example, whether the trussed roof is supported on external walls only, or there is a conventional roof bearing on internal load-bearing structure;

- identify main load-bearing structures;

- identify elements giving lateral restraint;

- identify how the loads are transferred to the ground and how the building is framed;

- consider whether the structures are flexible or rigid and how they are linked;

- record the structural condition and any significant movement in the walls and their openings, beams and lintels, floors, the roof framework and chimney stacks;

- assess the adequacy of the above ground structural framework and, if there is evidence of movement, determine its cause (whether above or below ground, structural, thermal or constructional) and identify the risks for the future;

- assess the likely condition of any foundations or footings from an above ground inspection and consider future risks;

- highlight defects and matters of concern.

It is important to make it clear to the client that older buildings were designed and constructed differently to modern buildings. This point is not just applicable to 'historic' buildings but to all buildings of a traditional type.

Works causing changes in the intended performance of a traditional building can have detrimental consequences on its condition, for example, the entrapment of moisture by impervious materials used in repair and maintenance such as cement-based renders, pointing, plasters and modern paints. Understanding how a building was intended to perform and changes to that performance is important in successfully determining a building's existing and future condition. The 'breathing' performance of all traditional buildings is important and the surveyor is advised to make full use of this section in order to explain the intended and existing performance.

6.5.2 *Structural frame*

This is an optional clause, for use if the building has a load-bearing frame (e.g. historic timber houses), or some forms of precast reinforced concrete (PRC). This may not be appropriate to modern timber-framed construction where the stud framework is best described as part of the wall structure.

6.5.3 *Main roof*

Externally, it is recommended that roof areas are inspected visually as closely as practicable using available equipment and safe vantage points. The interior of accessible roof voids should be inspected from the nearest safe vantage point to the extent practicable with the equipment available. Inaccessible voids should be noted and an opinion given by inference, with recommendation for further investigations if appropriate.

The following subheadings assume a pitched and tiled (or slated) roof:

- structure,
- coverings,
- valley gutters,
- rainwater goods,
- fascias, soffits and bargeboards,
- roof windows,
- parapets,
- flashings,
- ceilings, and
- insulation and ventilation.

Not all items in this list will always be relevant all of the time and adaptation may be required if, for example, the main roof is flat.

6.5.4 *Other roofs*

Depending upon their size, separate subheadings or paragraphs may be used for each roof or group of roofs, where considered significant, taking points in the same order as 'Main roof'.

Note that a balcony or roof terrace could perform, in part, the functions of a roof.

6.5.5 *Chimneys*

Chimneys can be reported separately or alongside either roofs or walls, to be decided by the surveyor in individual cases.

6.5.6 *External walls*

The exposed elements of all walls should be visibly inspected externally and internally where not obscured by heavy plant growth, furniture, fixed linings or finishes. The interior of wall cavities cannot normally be inspected except from formed access points. Wall foundations should only be opened up for inspection in cases where structural defects indicate problems below ground and on the specific instructions of the client and after prior approval of the property owner, confirmed in writing where appropriate.

6.5.7 *Damp-proof courses*

The type of damp-proof course, whether original or retrospectively installed, its effectiveness and its position relative to external ground level and internal floor level should be considered.

6.5.8 *Floor ventilation*

The surveyor is advised to consider the sufficiency of air bricks and/or grilles to provide sub-floor ventilation to suspended floors.

6.5.9 *Internal walls and partitions*

The constructional detail of the internal walls and partitions should be established to the extent possible by a surface inspection. Walls within construction voids should be inspected where accessible.

Surveyors are advised to include the following in their considerations:

- **Party walls**
  - Adequacy for fire separation, particularly in the roof void, should be noted.
  - If works are recommended, the surveyor should include relevant advice in respect of Party Wall legislation.

- **Load-bearing walls and partitions**
  - If previous load-bearing walls have been removed or altered, comment should be made on the apparent adequacy of support measures.

6.5.10 *Fireplaces and chimney breasts*

The surveyor is advised to comment on whether chimney breasts have been altered or removed and, if so, should also comment on the adequacy of support measures.

If flues are visible, the surveyor is advised to comment on jointing and the likely condition of any linings, etc.

Comment may need to be made on the condition of fireplaces and appliances.

6.5.11 *Basements/cellars*

The surveyor is recommended to comment upon the levels of ventilation, the presence of dampness and flooding, any drainage/pumping arrangements and the likelihood of tanking (original or subsequent) being present.

6.5.12 *Floors*

The surface of floors not covered with fixed floor coverings should be inspected as far as practicable. In the case of timber floors (where practicable and where permitted to do so), loose boards should be raised to enable the construction to be identified and their condition to be checked. Additionally, surveyors are advised to carry out a 'heel-drop check'. The surveyor may need to comment if joists are likely to be undersized, or defective. The surveyor is advised to comment on excessive deflections and general levels. Where necessary, separate advice can be provided by floor level (e.g. 'Ground floor' and 'Upper floors').

6.5.13 *Ceilings*

Inspect the ceilings from floor level.

6.5.14 *Windows, doors and joinery*

It is recommended that the surveyor checks joinery, where accessible from ground level externally, and open windows, where practicable, to examine vulnerable areas at closer quarters. Internally, attention may need to be paid to built-in cupboards, kitchen fitments, joinery near damp areas, solid floors and sanitary fittings.

Surveyors are advised to include the following in their considerations:

- windows,

- external doors,

- internal doors,

- stairs,

- skirtings and architraves,

- kitchen cupboards, and

- other fitted cupboards.

6.5.15 *Finishes and decorations*

This is a general commentary only. It may need to emphasise the importance of external decoration as protection to the building fabric.

6.5.16 *Dampness*

Dampness can occur for a variety of reasons (including rising damp, penetrating damp, trapped and displaced moisture, salt contamination, service leaks and condensation). Moisture may be on the surface of the fabric or concealed in the structure. The surveyor is recommended to check methodically for dampness visually and with a moisture meter at pertinent locations being mindful of how readings from such instruments may sometimes be affected by salts, metals or other conductive material. The surveyor is advised to suggest the likely origins of any dampness and to provide advice on how to overcome dampness that is considered (in the context of the building type) to be a problem to the building fabric and living conditions. The surveyor is not expected to conduct tests for salts or conduct calcium carbide tests unless this service is considered necessary by the surveyor and has been agreed with the client and the property owner (in the latter case, in writing). The surveyor is advised to warn the client of any risk that the presence of dampness may have caused problems such as rot in concealed timbers.

6.5.17 *Timber defects*

The surveyor is recommended to inspect exposed timbers, both externally and internally, for signs of rot or insect attack and should consider all aspects of the construction and condition including dampness, to assess the potential for damage to hidden timbers.

Similarly the surveyor may need to examine exposed timbers for the presence of active infestation by wood-boring insects and also determine the likelihood of infestation in the hidden structure. In both instances the surveyor is recommended to advise about remedial works.

6.5.18 *Structural movement*

Individual manifestations of structural movement will have been described for each element in the relevant section above. This section can be used to 'pull together' the surveyor's advice.

It is recommended that evidence of structural movement affecting the property or individual components is reported, including cracking, deflection, bulging, bowing and verticality. Given the circumstances of each case, the surveyor is advised to describe the evidence available and provide an opinion as to the most likely cause of the movement, whether the movement would seem to be recent or of long standing, and, in either case, whether it is thought to be continuing. It is recommended that advice is given as to whether or not repairs are necessary.

The report may also need to consider past remedial work and whether it has been effective.

6.6 Services

It is advisable that all building service installations, whether mains or privately supplied, are visually inspected to the extent sufficient for the surveyor to form an overall opinion on the type of installation, the materials used, its apparent age, its visible condition and the need for further investigation. The surveyor will **not** be expected to carry out testing of the installations or appliances other than normal operation in everyday use. The surveyor is not expected to perform or comment upon design calculations. The inspection should be carried out without the risk of causing injury to the surveyor or damage to the property. Where access is limited, this should be explained to the client. In respect of all services, the client should be advised that further tests would be required by appropriate specialists if assurance as to the condition or capability is required.

It is recommended that the following services are taken into account:

6.6.1 *Electrics*

The location and type of incoming supply, meter and switchgear, the nature of visible wiring, the availability of socket outlets and the nature of artificial lighting should be noted and reported on.

In view of the demands of computer equipment, the surveyor should not turn off the main electrical supply or test Residual Current Devices, except with the express permission of the property owner.

6.6.2 *Gas*

Surveyors are advised to describe the position of the gas service intake and meter and the location of outlets and appliances. It is recommended that they take account of the general siting of gas appliances, but they are not expected to carry out tests.

So far as gas is concerned, any smell of gas should be reported immediately to the occupier and the property owner or agent in order that appropriate action for the safety of property and persons may be taken.

6.6.3 *Water supply and plumbing*

The surveyor is advised to note and report on the nature of the installation including pipework, the entry point of supply, locations of internal and external stopcocks, the method of storage and the condition of sanitary fittings. It is recommended that taps are turned on and toilets flushed to check for general operation. References should be made to the general design and constructional aspects.

6.6.4 *Private water supplies*

The following may need to be considered:

- storage capacity,

- location,

- pumping and piping arrangements (and access thereto), and

- a laboratory check for potability.

6.6.5 *Hot water installations, boilers, control equipment, space heating, etc.*

It is advised that these services are inspected visually and where practicable, to check physical operation, the owner or occupier is asked to activate the central heating, air conditioning or mains switchgear. The report should note that the purpose of activating the system is to check basic operation and not to test its efficiency or safety. If, from what is apparent to the surveyor, he or she has safety concerns, these should be recorded with reasonable prominence and further investigations and suspension of use recommended.

6.6.6 *Drains*

The surveyor is advised to open all reasonably accessible, lightweight, inspection chamber covers within the curtilage of the property, record the assumed routes of the drain runs and report their general condition based upon a visual inspection. Where a water supply is available and turned on, the inspection may also involve running water through the system.

6.6.7 *Foul and surface water*

The surveyor is recommended to attempt to identify the means of foul and surface water disposal.

6.6.8 *Private drainage systems*

The following should be considered:

- type of system,

- location relative to watercourses and buildings,

- capacity relative to size of current building,

- pumping and piping arrangements (and access thereto),

- emptying and maintenance arrangements, and

- implications for replacement or repair relative to current criteria.

6.6.9 Other services

Other service installations may occasionally be found and should be subject to visual inspection, without testing. These may include:

- security alarms,
- smoke detectors,
- vacuum cleaning system,
- stairlift/handicapped hoist,
- remote control garage doors,
- warden call systems in sheltered developments,
- entry-phone system,
- communal lift,
- private electrical supply generators, and
- TV and radio installations.

The surveyor is advised to note:

- Electrical installations to swimming pools, plant and equipment would normally be specifically excluded and made the subject of specialist inspection and testing.

6.7 Environmental and other issues

6.7.1 Orientation and exposure

The impact of orientation upon the property should be clearly stated.

6.7.2 Thermal insulation and energy efficiency

The surveyor is advised to:

- describe the thermal shell of the building including external walls, windows, roofs, exposed floors and ground floors, taking into consideration the layout, location and orientation of the property and any porches or external lobbies;
- consider the nature of the heating system and heating controls;
- consider the nature of natural and artificial lighting and, where appropriate, advise upon the use of energy efficient bulbs; and
- provide advice on practical methods of upgrading insulation and on measures to reduce any associated risk of condensation.

6.7.3 Ventilation

The surveyor is advised to consider the availability of natural, passive and rapid ventilation to all habitable areas (including kitchens, bathrooms and shower rooms) and the ventilation of the building fabric.

6.7.4 *Noise and disturbance*

The surveyor is advised to consider the effect of noise from external sources on living conditions within the subject property and its grounds. Noise, for example, from aircraft, rail, traffic and other sources should be noted if it is significant at the time of inspection or could from inspection reasonably be anticipated. If a surveyor is instructed to consider a specific aspect (e.g. aircraft noise) the extent of the enquiries required should be agreed with the client. The sound insulation qualities of party structures may also need to be considered.

Any other possible nuisances, for example, smells that are known to or have become apparent to the surveyor whilst carrying out the inspection, should be noted.

6.7.5 *Means of escape*

The surveyor is advised to consider the size and height of the opening lights to all upper floor windows, access routes from all rooms and whether the access routes are closed or open. This is particularly of concern with open plan layouts and properties over two storeys high. Consideration of the adequacy of methods of protection to the means of escape in loft conversions and houses of three or more storeys is advisable. Surveyors may also need to consider providing advice in respect of fire resistance standards, for instance, in large, older houses within this category.

If considered appropriate, the introduction of smoke detectors outside kitchens and circulating areas at each floor level should be recommended.

6.7.6 *Other health and safety concerns*

Where the condition of the property, or its services, is so structurally weak or damp that it would be a health risk, appropriate advice should be given.

Features in the property, arising from inspection, that may pose a health and safety hazard, and any apparent health and safety issues are highlighted here or in the main body of the report.

6.7.7 *Hazardous materials*

The surveyor is recommended to provide advice where there is visual evidence of, or reasonable grounds to believe that, a material or technique has been used in the construction that is known to be hazardous to living conditions when worked upon, e.g. lead, asbestos or timber treatment.

6.7.8 *Security*

The surveyor is advised to consider basic security aspects affecting the property, e.g. the presence or lack of adequate window locks, door locks and alarm system.

6.8 Outbuildings, grounds and boundaries

6.8.1 *Gardens and grounds*

A brief general description of these features is required, and visible defects in paths, patios, steps, handrails, drives, etc. should be reported to the extent required by the agreed instructions.

6.8.2 *Garages, 6.8.3 Conservatories and 6.8.4 Other outbuildings*

The surveyor is advised to outline the construction and design and also report on any defects revealed by visual inspection. Any special client requirements in respect of anticipated usage should be considered.

Where the principal building is listed, it is advised that reference is made to the condition of all outbuildings and structures, including garden walls, likely to have been built before 1 July 1948.

6.8.5 *Boundaries*

Where identifiable, a general description of boundary fences, walls, and other structures should be given.

6.8.6 *Retaining walls*

The surveyor is advised to outline the construction and design, consider the consequence of failure and draw attention to any implications for household insurance and rebuilding cost. Any defects revealed by visual inspection should be described.

6.8.7 *Shared areas*

The extent of inspection actually carried out in shared areas and their general condition should be described.

Comments in respect of common services should be made under 'Services'.

6.9 Matters for legal advisor's attention

In addition to the legal advisor's usual pre-contract enquiries, legal issues may arise from the survey inspection itself. In such cases, the surveyor is advised to alert the client's legal advisor (if known and the client if not) to physical or other issues which could affect the property that may need investigation or clarification. Where the inspection reveals that there are areas of particular concern or relevance these should be appropriately highlighted.

The following paragraphs give examples of matters which might be referred to the legal advisor for consideration and the making of further enquiries.

6.9.1 *Statutory*

Examples of statutory matters might include:

- the need, in the case of buildings which might be listed or situated within a conservation area, for the status of the property to be established and a copy of any listing obtained;

- where trees are present which might be the subject of such orders, the existence and extent of any Tree Preservation Orders;

- planning consents and Building Regulation approvals – original compliance and/or consent for conversions, extensions, alterations or change of use and any particular works evident on inspection for which planning permission may have been required; and

- *Party Wall Act* – any known proposed works, extensions or repairs to the subject property and also works in progress on adjacent land and the need for the legal advisor to establish the existence of any Party Wall Agreements and/or Schedules of Condition, where appropriate, referring back to the surveyor as appropriate.

6.9.2 *Rights of way, easements and shared services*

Examples of issues to be described might include:

- tenure;

- flying freeholds or submerged freeholds;

- evidence of multiple occupation, tenancies or holiday lettings;

- evidence of possible trespass;

- evidence that suggests possible rights of way;

- arrangements in respect of private services;

- the adoption status of all abutting roads/footpaths;

- where private access roads or footways are present, the status of the rights of way and all maintenance/repairing liabilities;

- the availability and status of all service connections;

- rights of light;

- restrictions to occupation.

6.9.3 *Boundaries*

Boundary matters might include:

- evidence of poorly defined site boundaries.

6.9.4 *Environmental*

Examples of environmental matters might include:

- whether a Remediation Certificate exists for the site (e.g. new build on a previously contaminated site);

- through Local Authority Searches, whether the property is likely to be affected by adjacent, significant public or private developments;

- whether a Mining Search of the correct type is required.

6.9.5 *Guarantees/warranties*

Examples of guarantees/warranties might include:

- NHBC, Foundation 15 or Building Professional's Certificate for new build or conversion – it is important to establish the type of warranty offered and to verify the age of the property. The surveyor should draw the client's attention to the fact that builders' warranty schemes have limitations and that the terms should be carefully inspected;

- the availability and transferability of guarantees (e.g. in respect of underpinning, lateral restraint and chimney stabilisation works; timber and/or damp treatment works; cavity wall tie replacement works; double glazing; cavity wall insulation; remedial works to service installations, including re-lined drains, recent rewiring, replacement boilers, etc.; recent significant building repairs).

6.10 Additional services

Some clients may require additional information or advice on the property which lies outside the scope of the surveyor's usual building survey inspection and report. This presents an opportunity for surveyors with appropriate skills to provide additional services arising out of information obtained, conditions discovered or unexpected on-site restrictions on the scope of the inspection carried out.

It is essential that the client understands which services are standard and the additional services which may be available at extra cost.

The following list of additional services to suit client's special requirements is not exhaustive but is a menu of options that could be offered subject to the surveyor's experience, accreditation (where applicable) or resources within the practice. Where such services are subcontracted to others this should be clearly stated together with arrangements for payment of fees, costs, etc.

Surveyors are recommended to check with their professional indemnity insurers that suitable cover is in place for any additional services offered or supplied to the client, including situations where the client asks the surveyor to suggest the name or names of specialist contractors. If commissioning a test or report, the surveyor is advised to ensure that all subcontractors are directly employed by the client.

6.10.1 *Security issues*

In addition to the requirements to consider general security aspects the following additional services could be considered:

- security aspects of design – standard of locking devices, security, glazing, access to windows by way of flat roofs or adjoining structures, external lighting and access (surveyor); and

- internal security – specialist installations for integrated fire and security, telephone entry systems, etc. (specialist).

6.10.2 *Insurance rebuilding cost assessment*

Additional services could include:

- insurance rebuilding cost assessment using published BCIS indices; and

- more detailed assessments, in respect of non-standard properties, specialist properties, historic listed buildings, special or unusual forms of construction, finishes or installations, etc.

Information given to the client should explain the difference between an assessment of costs for insurance reinstatement and a valuation for other purposes. It would also be helpful to differentiate between the scope of services involved in the assessment of non-specialist properties and that required, for instance, for listed buildings where there is an obligation to repair or replace structures and materials on a like-for-like basis using conservation grade materials, techniques and workmanship. It should also be borne in mind that resources may not readily be available to implement repairs and that the works will usually take significantly longer at all stages.

6.10.3 *Valuation*

It is important to emphasise that the provisions of the *RICS Valuation and Appraisal Standards* (the 'Red Book') must be followed in respect of any valuation advice provided, including the need to establish for what purpose the valuation is required.

6.10.4 *Scale plans*

Some surveyors may include sketch floor plans to illustrate the layout, structure and defects. Scale plans are useful in cases where the client is considering alterations or extensions to the property but it is essential to establish for what purpose the plans are required. For example, floor plans for the identification of rooms to assist removal firms require far less accuracy than those for alterations, which are likely to require detailed measurements of room heights, headroom, etc.

Some estate agents now include floor plans in the property particulars. Whilst these can be quite accurate and sufficient for some purposes they should not be relied upon for more detailed requirements without a check for accuracy. Surveyors should use their own discretion in relation to the client's requirements and should explain the limitations of working with or from restricted survey data or data prepared by others. Surveyors should also be aware of the requirements of local authorities for properly prepared and reproduced plans drawn to a suitable scale for submission in connection with statutory applications.

6.10.5 *Testing of services*

Specialist tests of the building services installations should only be carried out with the property owner's prior approval and by known and suitably registered/accredited specialists.

Surveyors are advised to be prepared to comment upon specialist reports if requested to do so by the client.

6.10.6 *SAP rating report*

The Standard Assessment Procedure is a method of collation of information on the property for the purpose of measuring the overall energy efficiency. Only persons accredited by the government's authorised agents can undertake the inspections and obtain certified SAP ratings.

6.10.7 *Maintenance notes*

Many organisations already include standardised maintenance notes using generic information. The preparation of a property specific set of notes, cross-referenced to the survey report supplementing rather than duplicating or reducing the content of the report, may be very helpful to first time buyers or purchasers of listed or other old and possibly neglected buildings. The surveyor should, however, establish whether the client actually wants a survey report with maintenance notes or would be better served by a schedule of condition and/or a specification of work. It is for the surveyor to establish the precise requirements of the client.

6.10.8 *Feasibility studies*

The building survey is the ideal time to consider feasibility studies but the surveyor is advised to ensure that the consideration of projects does not interfere with the survey inspection – it should follow that inspection rather than being part of it. It is also essential to establish what the client's requirements are and whether the purchase of the property is dependent upon the ability to achieve their proposals. If the latter is the case then it might be more appropriate to recommend submission of a planning application (with all its attendant costs and delays) rather than to rely only upon a feasibility study untested by a full planning application.

6.10.9 *Further investigations*

The surveyor may recommend further investigations of parts of the structure or services where the level of inspection that he or she has been able to carry out is insufficient to form an opinion or to report adequately on some aspect where a defect is suspected. The recommendation should only be made when the trail cannot be followed further and the potential or suspected defect is of importance. The surveyor is advised to make a clear distinction between those further investigations that should be carried out before making an irrevocable decision to purchase (e.g. where extensive dry rot is suspected but not confirmed) and those that can reasonably be left until later (e.g. location and uncovering of manholes where other parts of the system are satisfactory).

The surveyor is advised to be wary of making recommendations for further investigations to be carried out by persons who have a financial interest in the implementation of their own advice or recommendations. Wherever possible all further investigations should be made by those who are qualified and/or experienced for the requisite task and who can illustrate that they can make recommendations that are free of any financial self-interest, e.g. from the sale of particular products or services.

Appendix A: Leasehold residential property

Any survey of leasehold residential property raises separate and additional factors arising from shared responsibilities and the wide variety of repairing covenants which are in common use. Particularly onerous repairing liabilities may exist quite independently of the subject property, for example, where the lease imposes a liability upon the property owner/occupier to pay a proportion of the total estate repair costs.

If the lease is not available before the inspection, the surveyor is advised to set out the limitations of any advice given.

The surveyor is recommended to:

- give advice in respect of relevant matters affecting the client's responsibility for effecting repairs, and liability to pay towards their cost, whether potential or in respect of existing wants of repair;

- advise the client to obtain independent legal advice on the interpretation of the lease;

- advise the client that the surveyor is not responsible for advising on the true legal effect of the lease which is the responsibility of the client's legal advisor upon whom the client must exclusively rely;

- advise that the possible rights and implications of lease renewal or enfranchisement have not been considered.

The surveyor is also advised to recommend that his or her client seek legal advice on the following questions, where appropriate.

a) Are the other flats occupied by long leaseholders or short leaseholders?

b) Is there a management company correctly set up and/or a managing agent appointed to deal with the running and maintenance of the block containing the property?

c) Does an appropriate annual maintenance and replacement fund exist, with suitable reserves, to deal with general cleaning, maintenance and repair of the common parts, and repairs to the main structure, centralised heating installation, lifts, etc?

d) What is the ground rent; what sum was last paid as a maintenance/service charge, and what period did it cover; and are any maintenance/service charge accounts satisfactory and up to date?

e) Is there evidence of regular maintenance of services; and are there satisfactory current certificates for the testing/servicing/maintenance of the following common services:

- the lifts;

- the fire escapes and fire alarms;

- the security system(s);

- any common water/heating system; and

- other communal facilities?

f) Are there any existing or foreseeable management problems or disputes, or any known outstanding repairs or programmed works, which would affect the level of the service/maintenance charge payable?

g) Is the liability clearly set out – as between the leaseholders, the freeholders and any management company – for repairs to the property, the common parts and the main structure; is the liability shared equally between leaseholders; and is there suitable machinery for settling any disputes which may arise in this area?

h) Is it the management company or each individual leaseholder that is responsible for the building insurance, and is there a block insurance policy?

i) Are there any unusual restrictions on the occupation or sale of the property?

Appendix B: Example Terms and Conditions of Engagement

Particulars

The Client: (Name)
                   (Address)

The Surveyor: (Name)
                   (Address)

The Property:

Purpose of the Report:

Details of any special instructions:

Likely inspection date:

Likely Report delivery date:

Number of copy Reports to be provided:

Agreed Fee (inclusive of VAT): £

Additional Fees (inclusive of VAT): £

Payment Date:

Signature(s) of Client(s) to confirm acceptance of Terms and Conditions of Engagement

Specific terms

1. **Description of the Property to be inspected**

2. **Additional services (if applicable)**

    2.1   Testing of services (if applicable)

    2.2   Additional investigation (if applicable)

    The Client will obtain the Property owner's consent to, and the Surveyor will carry out, the following additional investigations: [insert]

    2.3   Arboricultural Report (if applicable)

    2.4   Costed estimates for repairs (if applicable)

    2.5   Market valuation (if applicable)

2.6　Insurance rebuilding cost assessment (if applicable)

3.　Special Terms Agreed (if applicable)

3.1　[Record any special terms agreed]

General terms

1.　Introduction

a. This document sets out the contractual terms upon which the Surveyor will advise the Client by means of a written report as to his or her opinion of the visible condition and state of repair of the Property.

b. The individual carrying out the inspection and providing advice will be a chartered surveyor.

c. The Surveyor will use all of the care and skill to be reasonably expected of an appropriately experienced chartered surveyor.

2.　Content of the Report

In accordance with these terms the Surveyor will report upon:

a. the main aspects of the Property including assessing the site/location, the design, structural framework, fabric and services;

b. the grounds, boundaries and environmental aspects considered to affect the Property;

c. any requirements for further investigation arising from the inspection.

3.　Delivery of the Report

a. The Report is to be delivered by the date agreed or at such later date as is reasonable in the circumstances.

b. The Surveyor will send the Report to the Client's address (or other agreed address) by first class post for the sole use of the Client. The Client agrees to keep the Report confidential disclosing its contents only to the Client's professional advisors. In particular (but without limit) the Client must not disclose the whole or any part of the Report to any person (other than a professional advisor) who may intend to rely upon it for the purpose of any transaction.

4.　Payment of fees

a. The Client will pay the Agreed Fee, any Additional Fees, any VAT and any agreed disbursements by the Payment Date.

b. The Client will be liable for interest on any late payment at the rate of 8% p.a. above the Bank of England base rate current at the date of the relevant fee account.

5. Assumptions

Unless otherwise expressly agreed the Surveyor while preparing the Report will assume that:

a. the property (if for sale) is offered with vacant possession;

b. the Property is connected to mains services with appropriate rights on a basis that is known and acceptable to the Client; and

c. access to the Property is as of right upon terms known and acceptable to the Client.

6. Scope of the inspection

a. Generally

i.   The Surveyor will consider his or her advice carefully but is not required to advise on any matter the significance of which in relation to the Property is not apparent at the time of inspection from the inspection itself.

ii. The Surveyor will inspect diligently but is not required to undertake any action which would risk damage to the Property or injury to him- or herself.

iii. The Surveyor will not undertake any structural or other calculations.

b. Accessibility

i.   The Surveyor will inspect as much of the internal and external surface area of the building as is practicable but will not inspect those areas which are covered, unexposed or not reasonably accessible from within the site, or adjacent public areas.

ii. The Surveyor is not required to move any obstruction to inspection including, but not limited to, furniture and floor coverings.

c. Floors

The Surveyor will lift accessible sample loose floorboards and trap doors, if any, which are not covered by heavy furniture, ply or hardboard, fitted carpets or other fixed floor coverings. The Surveyor will not attempt to cut or lift fixed floorboards without express permission of the owner.

d. Fixed covers or housings

The surveyor will not attempt to remove securely fixed covers or housings without the express permission of the owner.

e. Roofs

The Surveyor will inspect the roof spaces if there are available hatches which are not more than three metres above the adjacent floor or ground. Where no reasonable access is available, the roof spaces will not be inspected. Similarly, outer surfaces of the roof or adjacent areas will be inspected using binoculars, but will be excluded if they cannot be seen.

f. **Boundaries, grounds and outbuildings**

The inspection will include boundaries, grounds and permanent outbuildings but will not include constructions or equipment with a specific leisure purpose including, without limit, swimming pools or tennis courts.

g. **Services**

The Surveyor will carry out a visual inspection of the service installations where accessible. Drainage inspection covers will be lifted where they are accessible and it is safe and practicable to do so. No tests of the service installations will be carried out unless previously agreed, although general overall comments will be made where possible and practicable. The Surveyor will report if it is considered that tests are advisable.

h. **Areas not inspected**

The Surveyor will identify any areas which would normally be inspected but which he or she was unable to inspect.

i. **Flats or maisonettes**

Unless otherwise agreed, the Surveyor will inspect only the subject flat and garage (if any), the related internal and external common parts and the structure of the building or particular block in which the subject flat is situated. Other flats will not be inspected. The Surveyor will state in the Report the limits of access and/or visibility in relation to the common parts and structure. The Surveyor will state whether he or she has seen a copy of the lease and, if not, the assumptions as to repairing obligations on which he or she is working.

j. **Environmental and other issues**

i.   Particular noise and disturbance affecting the Property will only be noted if it is significant at the time of the inspection or if specific investigation has been agreed between the Surveyor and the Client and confirmed in writing.

ii. The Surveyor will report on any obvious health and safety hazards to the extent that they are apparent from elements of the Property considered as part of the inspection.

7.   Hazardous materials

a.   Unless otherwise expressly stated in the Report, the Surveyor will assume that no deleterious or hazardous materials or techniques have been used in the construction of the Property. However, the Surveyor will advise in the Report if, in his or her view, there is a likelihood that deleterious material has been used in the construction and specific enquiries should be made or tests should be carried out by a specialist.

b.   Subject to clause 6b the Surveyor, based upon a limited visual inspection, will note and advise upon the presence of lead water supply pipes and asbestos.

c. The Surveyor will advise in the Report if the Property is in an area where, based on information published by the National Radiological Protection Board, there is a risk of radon. In such cases the Surveyor will advise that tests should be carried out to establish the radon level.

d. The Surveyor will advise if there are transformer stations or overhead power lines which might give rise to an electro-magnetic field, either over the subject Property or visible immediately adjacent to the Property. The Surveyor is not required to assess any possible effect on health or to report on any underground cables.

8. Ground conditions

The Surveyor will not be required to comment upon the possible existence of noxious substances, landfill or mineral extraction, or other forms of contamination.

9. Consents, approvals and searches

a. The Surveyor will be entitled to assume that the Property is not subject to any unusual or onerous restrictions, obligations or covenants which apply to the Property or affect the reasonable enjoyment of the Property.

b. The Surveyor will be entitled to assume that all planning, Building Regulations and other consents required in relation to the Property have been obtained. The Surveyor will not verify whether such consents have been obtained. Any enquiries should be made by the Client or the Client's legal advisers. Drawings and specifications will not be inspected by the Surveyor unless otherwise previously agreed.

c. The Surveyor will be entitled to assume that the Property is unaffected by any matters which would be revealed by a Local Search and replies to the usual enquiries, or by a Statutory Notice, and that neither the Property, nor its condition, its use or its intended use, is or will be unlawful.

10. Insurance rebuilding cost assessment

The Surveyor will provide an insurance rebuilding cost assessment only if this is agreed at the time of taking instructions. Building insurance cost assessments will be calculated using the current edition of the BCIS *Guide to House Rebuilding Costs*.

11. Additional services

The Surveyor will provide, for an additional fee, such additional services as may be specified in the Specific Terms or are agreed between the Surveyor and the Client and confirmed by the Surveyor in writing.

12. Miscellaneous

a. In the event of a conflict between these General Terms and the Specific Terms, the Specific Terms prevail.

b. Unless expressly provided, no term in the agreement between the

Surveyor and the Client is enforceable under the *Contracts (Rights of Third Parties) Act* 1999 by any person other than the Surveyor or the Client.

c. Where the Client has instructed the Surveyor to make investigations which cause damage to the Property on the basis that the Client has obtained the owner's consent, the Client will indemnify the Surveyor against any loss or cost arising.

d. **Dispute Resolution**   In the event that the Client has a complaint regarding the standard of service he or she has received, a formal complaints handling procedure will be followed. A copy of the Surveyor's complaints handling procedure is available upon request. Using the Surveyor's complaints handling procedure will not affect the Client's legal rights.

e. The Client may only rely upon the Surveyor's advice and Report for purposes described in the Particulars or communicated to the Surveyor in writing prior to the agreement of the Fee and if the client wishes to rely upon such advice and Report for any other purpose he or she may only do so with the written consent of the Surveyor.

Further reading and information

Copies of Appendix B: *Example Terms and Conditions of Engagement* can be obtained in packs of 20 from RICS Books at www.ricsbooks.com

RICS official materials

Surveying safely, RICS Construction Faculty, 2002
(www.rics.org/resources/surveying_safely/index.html)

The following RICS official materials are available from www.ricsbooks.com

Asbestos, RICS guidance note, RICS Books, Coventry, 2003
(ISBN 1 84219 063 6)

Building Maintenance: Strategy Planning and Procurement, RICS guidance note, RICS Books, Coventry, 2000 (ISBN 0 85406 977 1)

Contamination and Environmental Matters: Their implications for property professionals, RICS guidance note (2nd edition), RICS Books, Coventry, 2003 (ISBN 1 84219 130 6)

Party Wall Legislation & Procedure, RICS guidance note (5th edition), RICS Books, Coventry, 2002 (ISBN 1 84219 073 3)

Practice Management: guidelines for surveyors, RICS guidance note, RICS Books, Coventry, 2003 (ISBN 1 84219 136 5)

The Red Book: RICS Appraisal and Valuation Standards (5th edition) (loose-leaf), RICS Books, Coventry, 2003 (ISBN 1 84219 123 3)

The Red Book: RICS Appraisal and Valuation Standards (5th edition) (online), RICS Books, Coventry, 2003 (ISBN 1 84219 124 1)

BCIS publications

The following BCIS cost guides are also available from www.ricsbooks.com – these guides are reproduced each year with updated data:

BCIS Guide to House Rebuilding Costs 2003, BCIS Limited, London, 2003 (ISBN 1 90085 884 3)

BCIS Guide to House Rebuilding Costs 2003 Regional Supplement, BCIS Limited, London, 2003 (ISBN 1 90085 885 1)

BCIS Guide to Rebuilding Costs of Flats 2003, BCIS Limited, London, 2003 (ISBN 1 90085 886 X)

A new guide is due to be published in the spring of 2004 which will provide guidance on typical costs of repairs identified in residential surveys.